United Kingdom

Tradition, Culture, and Daily Life

MAJOR NATIONS IN A GLOBAL WORLD

Books in the Series

United Kingdom

Tradition, Culture, and Daily Life

MAJOR NATIONS IN A GLOBAL WORLD

Richard Garratt

Mason Crest

Mason Crest
450 Parkway Drive, Suite D
Broomall, PA 19008
www.masoncrest.com

Printed and bound in the United States of America.

First printing
9 8 7 6 5 4 3 2 1

Series ISBN: 978-1-4222-3339-9
ISBN: 978-1-4222-3351-1
ebook ISBN: 978-1-4222-8591-6

The Library of Congress has cataloged the hardcopy format(s) as follows:

Library of Congress Cataloging-in-Publication Data

Garratt, Richard.
  United Kingdom / by Richard Garratt.
   pages cm. -- (Major nations in a global world: tradition, culture, and daily life)
  Includes index.

  ISBN 978-1-4222-3351-1 (hardback) -- ISBN 978-1-4222-3339-9 (series) -- ISBN 978-1-4222-8591-6 (ebook)
 1. Great Britain--Juvenile literature. 2. Great Britain--Description and travel--Juvenile literature. 3. Great Britain--Social life and customs--Juvenile literature. I. Title.
  DA632.G38 2015
  941--dc23
                                        2015010457

Developed and produced by MTM Publishing, Inc.
        Project Director   Valerie Tomaselli
        Copyeditor   Lee Motteler/Geomap Corp.
        Editorial Coordinator Andrea St. Aubin

Indexing Services   Andrea Baron, Shearwater Indexing

Art direction and design by Sherry Williams, Oxygen Design Group

Contents

KEY ICONS TO LOOK FOR:

Words to Understand: These words with their easy-to-understand definitions will increase the reader's understanding of the text, while building vocabulary skills.

Sidebars: This boxed material within the main text allows readers to build knowledge, gain insights, explore possibilities, and broaden their perspectives by weaving together additional information to provide realistic and holistic perspectives.

Research Projects: Readers are pointed toward areas of further inquiry connected to each chapter. Suggestions are provided for projects that encourage deeper research and analysis.

Text-Dependent Questions: These questions send the reader back to the text for more careful attention to the evidence presented there.

Series Glossary of Key Terms: This back-of-the book glossary contains terminology used throughout this series. Words found here increase the reader's ability to read and comprehend higher-level books and articles in this field.

The Tower of London viewed from across the Thames.

INTRODUCTION

The current country of the United Kingdom of Great Britain and Northern Ireland—often referred to simply as the UK or Britain—has existed as a unified sovereign state for a very short time—only since 1927, in fact. The seeds of the union were sewn in 1707 when the kingdoms of England and Scotland merged into a country called Great Britain and later, in 1800, the Kingdom of Ireland joined to create the United Kingdom of Great Britain and Ireland. However, in 1922, Ireland seceded from the UK and became the Irish Free State. One day later, Northern Ireland seceded from the new Ireland to rejoin the United Kingdom, with the present formal name coming into being a few years later, in 1927. So, like the United States—although with countries instead of states—England, Wales, Scotland, and Northern Ireland are united under a central government and currency but with its individual countries able to make decisions that concern themselves.

Tiny geographically in comparison to other nations, the UK has had an extensive and enduring influence on the world. Through its imperial strategies of acquiring colonies and harnessing their economic life to the mainland, Britain has enjoyed the produce and resources of countries around the world while bolstering its own economy. Being an island, its inhabitants across the centuries have taken to the seas on long voyages of exploration, thus ensuring the name Great Britain was known around the globe.

Its storied landscape is punctuated with castles, quaint villages, and churches. Its many canals criss-crossing the countryside and connecting its towns and cities are a testament to the Industrial Revolution born in the kingdom. Its miles of coastline—with its ports as well as its beauty—have inspired artists and writers who have helped define Western civilization and have urged its inhabitants to look outward beyond its shores.

Changing of the Guard at
Buckingham Palace, 2013.

WORDS TO UNDERSTAND

dictatorial: expecting unquestioning obedience.

excommunicated: banished by a religious community.

regnal: relating to royalty.

virulently: contagiously.

CHAPTER 1

History, Religion, and Tradition

The lands of United Kingdom have been populated for thousands of years. Some of the earliest evidence of human activity has been left in stone: farmers arrived from Europe around 3,000 years BCE, erecting the first stone circles, the most famous of which is Stonehenge.

Following an initial invasion headed by Julius Caesar in 55 BCE, the Romans had occupied England, Wales, and Scotland by 140 CE. After over 400 years of rule, the Romans withdrew from Britain leaving an enduring legacy, including an extensive road network; water supply, sewage, and sanitation systems; and the foundations of many of the country's major cities.

The monument known as Stonehenge was once thought to be incomplete, but a dry summer in 2014 revealed the remaining stones that completed the circle.

With the Romans gone, the country had no strong army to defend itself. Tribes called the Angles, Saxons, and Jutes rowed across the North Sea from their homelands to settle in Britain. In 793 another invasion began: the Vikings arrived from Scandinavia and took Northumbria in the north, as well as eastern England.

In 1066 the English army marched to Hastings on the south coast to take on the forces of the Normans from France, led by William Duke of Normandy (later known as William the Conqueror), who defeated the English. William became king of England that year and ruled until 1087. The House of Normandy reigned until 1135 when it was succeeded by the House of Blois, followed by the House of Plantagenet.

 ROYAL NUMBERS

It was only after William the Conqueror (William I) that Britain started using **regnal** numbers to distinguish monarchs from others with the same name. Before 1066, kings were known by nicknames such as Aethelred "the Unready," who was son of Edgar "the Peaceful," or Sweyn "Forkbeard," the son of Harald "Bluetooth." Even William I was sometimes known by his nickname, "William the Bastard"!

Starting with Henry II in 1154, the House of Plantagenet, also called the House of Anjou, was unusual in that the kings ruled from France. The Angevins included Richard I—"the Lionheart"—who was a great warrior and military leader. By the age of sixteen he was in command of his own army. He earned his nickname when he was central commander in the Third Crusade (1189–1192), an attempt to reconquer the Holy Land taken by Muslim forces some ten to twenty years earlier.

The rival houses of Lancaster and York succeeded the Plantagenets, although all carried the male bloodline from Henry II. Their rivalry led to the Wars of the Roses (1455–1487), so named because the heraldic badge for each included a rose: a red one for the Lancasters and a white for the Yorks. The monarchy changed from Lancastrian to Yorkist, back to Lancaster, and then to York again. This long line of monarchs came to an end in 1485 when Richard III was defeated in the Battle of Bosworth by Henry VII, a Tudor. The Tudors, including the famous Henry VIII, were a Welsh-English family, reigning for nearly 120 years.

Henry VIII is best known for having six wives in the thirty-eight years of his reign. In his quest to father a male heir, he fell out with the Catholic Church over his plans to marry his second wife, Anne Boleyn. When he was **excommunicated** by the pope in 1533, he appointed himself supreme head of the Church of England.

Elizabeth I, the daughter of Henry VIII and Anne Boleyn, ruled for forty-five years, during which time Sir Francis Drake circumnavigated the world; the English defeated the Spanish Armada, a fleet of 130 warships attempting to overthrow the queen; William Shakespeare's first play was performed; and the East India Company, Britain's first involvement with India, was established. After she died childless, her cousin James VI of Scotland succeeded to the English throne as James I of England.

Portrait of Henry VIII by Hans Holbein the Younger, oil on canvas (ca. 1537).

THE BLACK DEATH

The Black Death, or bubonic plague, ravaged England several times, the first being in June 1348. Originating in China, it spread quickly and **virulently**: it reached London by the summer of 1349, and by the time it receded in December it had killed half of the population. It returned twelve years later, killing 20 percent of the already hugely diminished population and then intermittently until the Great Plague of London in 1665–1666.

James I, a Protestant like Elizabeth, hoped to improve relations with Catholics, but the divide became worse after an unsuccessful attempt by Catholic extremists to blow up the Houses of Parliament. James's successor, Charles I, was keen to unify Britain and Ireland, but his handling of Parliament actually led to the English Civil War (1642–1651), between supporters of Parliament and the monarchy. The monarchy was replaced with the Protectorate under the **dictatorial** rule of Oliver Cromwell, one of the main commanders of the Parliamentarian army. Two years after his death in 1658, the monarchy was restored.

Through his Portuguese wife, Charles II (the "Merry Monarch") acquired Tangiers in northern Africa and Bombay in India, thus laying the foundations of the British Empire. India and parts of the empire would be held by Britain until the middle of the twentieth century.

While the Black Death is believed to have killed around 80,000 people, it is suggested that the Great Fire of London in September of 1666 actually saved lives by burning down unsanitary buildings in which rats and fleas transmitted the plague.

Charles II (the "Merry Monarch"), a patron of the arts and science, founded the Royal Society and sponsored the architect Christopher Wren, who built some of England's greatest edifices. This image shows St. Paul's Cathedral, designed by Wren and completed in 1708.

In 1714 George of Hanover, the capital of Lower Saxony, a region in central Germany, came to rule the United Kingdom. George could speak no English, and he appointed a prime minister, Robert Walpole, to help him communicate. From this moment on, all future monarchs would take a much more passive role, leaving the running of the government to the prime minister.

George III, third to reign in the house of Hanover, came to the throne during the Seven Years' War (actually spanning ten years, 1754–1763, but with the main conflict starting in 1756), fought among European powers to control their growing empires across the world. During his reign, the British Empire spread across the globe, with territories in the Caribbean, North America, Australia and New Zealand, Africa, India, and Southeast Asia.

This period also saw the beginning of the Industrial Revolution, which transformed British life with a new style of mechanized work made possible by the steam engine. Starting around 1760, entire industries and areas of human life, such as textile manufacturing, mining, and transportation, were revolutionized.

THE INDUSTRIAL REVOLUTION

One of the reasons the Industrial Revolution started in Britain was that it had large reserves of coal, used to power steam engines and other machines, and iron ore, used to produce steel. Its colonies helped as well: they supplied not just raw materials but a marketplace for the finished products.

Queen Victoria came to power at the age of eighteen in 1837 on the heels of the Industrial Revolution. Very inexperienced in politics, she relied heavily on her prime minister, Lord Melbourne. She married Albert, a German from a family connected to many of Europe's monarchs, in 1840, thereby unifying Britain's fortunes to another important European power. During her nearly sixty-four-year reign—the longest of any British monarch—she ruled a quarter of the world's population.

After Victoria's death in 1901, the German line that inherited the throne would take the name of Windsor as anti-German feelings took hold during World War I. The Windsor's reign lasts until the present day with, at the time of writing, Elizabeth II still queen after sixty-two years.

During the Windsor's rule, the United Kingdom was tied more than ever to world affairs. In 1914 it entered World War I, also called the Great War, on the side of France, Russia, and other Triple Entente allies. It fought against Germany in World War II, during which it lost over 450,000 lives and suffered great damage. However, the country—with its Allies including the United States—emerged from the war victorious.

In the postwar years, the United Kingdom has maintained its central role in international politics and its cultural vibrancy remains ever strong, especially due to the contributions of immigrants from its former colonies. Even as its economy has lost some of its legendary vitality, it remains a center of economic and cultural life in a globalizing world.

In 1850, Queen Victoria's husband Albert organized the Great Exhibition, an event showcasing the world's advances in science, technology, and the arts.

TEXT-DEPENDENT QUESTIONS

1. What were some of the contributions of the Roman Empire during its settlement of Britain?
2. Who was Henry VIII?
3. What country did the United Kingdom fight against in World War II?

RESEARCH PROJECTS

1. Use the library and Internet to prepare a timeline of one of the monarchs discussed in the chapter.
2. Investigate the development of the steam engine and its influence in the Industrial Revolution. Write a short essay to present your findings.

All Saints Church at Great Chalfield near Melksham in Wiltshire, England.

Friends relaxing together in one of London's many parks.

WORDS TO UNDERSTAND

comportment: the way someone carries themselves and behaves.

deadpan: without emotion or expression.

demeanor: someone's overall look and attitude.

innuendo: an indirect (and usually malicious) implication.

macabre: extremely strange in an eerie way.

CHAPTER 2

Family and Friends

Asense of belonging is extremely important in the UK, and despite recent changes, the family is still a defining element of British society. That said, with many of Britain's families moving apart and away from their "home" town—in search of employment or perhaps a further education—friendship is becoming more and more important.

Seeking further education, many women now delay starting a family or simply do not have any children at all. One-fifth of women are now childless at age forty-five, and 45 percent of families have just one child. The country's tax and financial systems encourage this. Unlike in France, for instance, where the tax structure encourages families to have more children, the UK gives a greater child allowance for the firstborn than any subsequent child. High house prices and growing unemployment are forcing more and more young adults to live with their parents. Some now never leave in the first place. As of 2013, over a quarter of twenty- to thirty-four-year-olds live with their parents, sometimes leading to friction in the family.

The average overall life expectancy in Britain is eighty-one years, but many people live much longer. Most older folks live on their own, as family members have moved away, but often younger family members must make the difficult decision to use residential care homes, which are usually chosen within relatively easy reach of at least one family member.

 THE CLASS SYSTEM

The British class system has been changing, with increasing upward and downward mobility, greater access to higher education, and a change in wealth distribution. However, the class system still exists and the differences are noticed in such things as accent, manners, **comportment**, and **demeanor**. Indeed, Britons still find it easy to detect someone's class!

The British are usually thought of as reserved and polite. Even among family members, greeting females with one kiss to the cheek is sufficient and a handshake among males is the norm. The greeting "How do you do" is not a question and should be answered with "How do you do" as well! Informal greetings are "Hello" or "Hi," and when saying goodbye you often hear "Cheers." The same word can be used to mean "Thank you." The British also like to form queues (standing in line), and pushing in front is frowned upon. If someone accidentally bumps into another person, they will probably both say "Sorry," even the person who is not at fault!

The British tend not to be very animated when they speak and do not use superlatives. However, this doesn't mean that they are emotionless, just that they feel being reserved is appropriate in public. And even behind closed doors it is considered rude to ask personal questions. "How much do you earn?"; "How old are you?"; and "Where are you from?" would all be thought of as impolite.

Lasting friendships are quite often made at school, a phenomenon made easier with the social networking sites available on the Internet. Friends can also be made in the workplace, and it is not unusual to "have a quick pint down the pub" after work. This applies to both sexes and is often on a Friday evening before setting off home for the weekend. Another way to make friends is by joining a club or participating in a sport.

An inside view of a London pub.

A lot has been said about Britain's drinking culture. Britons seem to be able to **quaff** large amounts of alcohol, partly due to the licensing laws. A person must be over the age of eighteen to be able to purchase alcoholic beverages, whether they are to be consumed at home or at a pub or bar. However, they are allowed to drink at home or other private premises from the age of five.

Unfortunately, according to many, the British pub—once a center of British social life—is in decline, with twenty-eight closing every week, according to some sources. This is due to a variety of causes: the effectiveness of the drunk-driving campaign and the fact that supermarkets sell discount beer, wine, and liquor. Even so, the traditional British pub can still be found in large numbers.

When a group of friends meets, the new arrival will generally say "hi" or "hello" to the group, unlike in most of continental Europe where everyone is acknowledged in turn. It is not considered impolite to make this general greeting, which allows conversations to continue quickly after a new arrival. A recent habit, particularly among the younger generation, is for everyone to place their mobile telephone on the table in front of them and to make and answer calls whether or not they are already in conversation with their friends.

 ## THE BRITISH SENSE OF HUMOR

The British are renowned for their understated sense of humor filled with self-deprecation and sarcasm. Jokes are often recounted with a **deadpan** delivery and can be told about virtually any subject with no taboos, apart from, perhaps, racism. **Innuendo**, satire, absurdity, and a sense of **macabre** are typical in anecdotes and in comedy programs on TV.

Weekends are a special time for both families and friends. Often both parents will have worked a five-day week, leaving Saturday to do the family shopping. Not long ago, shops were not allowed to open on a Sunday; now, however, the day is treated the same as any other but with more limited hours of operation. Sunday is traditionally the day when people practicing a faith would go to church. Britain is now so multicultural that it is becoming less Christian, and fewer people regularly attend a church, preferring to spend the day with family and friends. The weekends are also days to catch up on gardening, household chores, and do-it-yourself projects.

In fact, the country has long been known for its love of gardening. There is an expression, "an Englishman's home is his castle," and the garden surrounding it is part of this. A lot of rivalry—usually good natured—might exist among neighbors about who can produce the best kept garden. Britons can be quite eccentric, and this manifests itself in the garden design, including the use of small figurines such as the garden gnome.

A garden gnome.

THE GARDEN GNOME

Although first made in Germany, garden gnomes—small figurines, usually wearing a pointed hat—came to Britain in 1847, when Sir Charles Isham brought twenty-one back from a trip to Germany. One remains at the original house and is insured for £1 million ($1.5 million)!

Visitors in the Waterlily House at the Royal Botanic Gardens in Kew, London.

Vacations are a part of leisure time and an important opportunity to bond as a family. Sometimes one parent may commute a long distance to work, leaving home early and returning late, and the annual family holiday can be the only time, apart from weekends, they can spend any length of time with their children. During economic downturns, especially the one beginning in 2008, families have remained in Britain for the vacation, taking a "staycation" as it is known.

Of course, family holidays are changing in step with the changes in families. The once typical British family of two parents and their children is gradually being replaced by single-parent households. In 1970, 18 percent of families were headed by a lone parent, but it is estimated that by 2020 there will be more single people than married, with around 40 percent of children being born to cohabiting parents. Following changes in legislation in England and Wales, same-sex marriages were legalized in March 2014, while in Scotland it was December of the same year, although same-sex couples have had the right to adopt children since 2002. Indeed, the stereotypical image of a family is ever changing.

Beachgoers enjoy the giant display of bubbles in Portmeirion, North Wales.

TEXT-DEPENDENT QUESTIONS

1. How has the family structure changed in the United Kingdom in the past several decades?

2. Describe the typical British sense of humor.

3. Describe how typical Britons spend their time on the weekends.

RESEARCH PROJECTS

1. Use the library and Internet to research family structures in the UK, the United States, and another country. Develop a table comparing specific features—such as size of households, number of children, single or married parents, and the like—across the three countries.

2. Collect photos of garden gnomes and other figurines from the Internet, with a focus on those in Britain. Make a photo collage, using captions that state where the garden is, what the figurine represents, and other interesting features of the garden.

Fans show their British pride during the London Olympic Games in 2012.

Beef Wellington, a traditional British dish.

WORDS TO UNDERSTAND

distillery: a facility that makes liquors, including whiskey.

frangipane: a sponge-like filling made with ground almonds.

homogenization: the process of blending elements together, sometimes resulting in a less interesting mixture.

savory: salty in taste, as opposed to sweet.

suet: fat from beef or mutton (an older sheep).

CHAPTER **3**

Food and Drink

Given the long geographic reach of the British Empire, as well as post–World War II immigration, Britain is a cultural melting pot, made evident by the types of food that are eaten. Of course, traditional British pies and puddings are still to be found, but so are stir-fries of Thai and Chinese origin and curries from India and Pakistan. In fact, the well-known Indian dish chicken tikka masala is the most popular dish in the country.

The traditional "full English breakfast"—sausage, bacon, eggs, and other side dishes—is now more of a specialty. Breakfast nowadays is of cereals, such as cornflakes, toast and marmalade, and the ever-present tea or coffee.

A "full English breakfast"—consisting of bacon, sausage, and eggs, often accompanied by fried bread, tomatoes, black pudding (a sausage made from pork blood and oatmeal), mushrooms, and baked beans.

Available all over Britain, but more commonly in Scotland, a filling and healthy start to the day can be found in a bowl of porridge. This consists of crushed oats boiled in either milk or water (or a mixture of both) and made with either salt, for a savory dish, or sugar or honey for a sweet dish.

PUDDING FOR DESSERT?

For Americans in Britain, the term "pudding" can be confusing. It refers both to dessert of any kind as well as a dish made in the style of an American pudding, the thick creamy dessert cooked on a stove and cooled before serving—but one that is either sweet or **savory**.

In the past, the midday meal was the most substantial of the day, allowing workers a break and giving them strength to continue during the afternoon, though with many people taking shorter lunches or traveling long distances to work, the meal often consists of sandwiches, possibly a pork pie, a packet of crisps (called potato chips in American English), and a piece of fruit. The evening meal tends to be the largest of the day, comprising a starter, main course, dessert, and possibly cheese.

Different regions or counties have their own specialties, often named after the county or town from which they originated. A Lancashire Hot Pot, from the northwest coast of England, is a slow-cooked casserole of lamb, onions, and carrots. Caerphilly Pie is a Welsh recipe using chicken; leeks, which are the national emblem of Wales; prunes; and Caerphilly cheese, a white, crumbly, sharp-tasting cheese.

A MINER'S MEAL

Cornish pasties, associated with Cornwall, the westernmost county in England, are handheld pies filled with chopped meat, diced potatoes and carrots, and onions. Traditionally, tin miners ate them as a nourishing and convenient lunch, one that could be easily eaten in the mine or at the surface, without having to wash their hands too much.

Traditional Cornish pasties.

Haggis, the national dish of Scotland, is made from sheep's offal (the liver, heart, and lungs—the bits often thrown away), which is cooked, mixed with oatmeal and **suet**. This mixture is put inside the sheep's stomach, sewn up, and boiled for about three hours. In Yorkshire, a county in northern England, roast meat and gravy is served either with or in a Yorkshire pudding, which is made from a batter consisting of flour, milk, and eggs.

Other traditional dishes include shepherd's pie and cottage pie. Both use minced meat with diced carrots and peas, along with a topping of puréed potato, but shepherd's pie uses lamb and cottage pie uses beef. Toad in the hole is a recipe using pork sausages cooked in the same batter mix as Yorkshire pudding and served with an onion gravy—not some horror dish made from amphibians!

Traditional desserts include spotted dick, a suet pudding with raisins or currants and served with custard, and bread and butter pudding, a recipe using leftover stale bread, spread with butter, and baked with raisins or sultanas in a milk and cream sauce. There are regional favorites as well, such as Bakewell tart from a town in Derbyshire,

A traditional Sunday lunch of roast beef and Yorkshire pudding with gravy.

toward the north of England, which is made from a pastry base, spread with raspberry jam and with a **frangipane** filling baked in the oven. Malvern pudding from the town of the same name in Worcestershire, bordering England and Wales, is a baked dish made with apples covered with egg custard topped with butter, sugar, and cinnamon.

THE SUNDAY ROAST

The "Sunday roast" has been served throughout the United Kingdom—most often in the middle of the day—and can be a joint of beef, pork, lamb, or a whole chicken or turkey. This is accompanied by roast potatoes, at least one vegetable, and, of course, gravy. Usually there is the ritual of carving the meat at the table and serving it in order—from the youngest member of the family to the oldest.

"Take-out" meals are very popular in Britain as they are convenient and also give people the opportunity to eat recipes from many cultures. Some have been around for a long time, such as "fish and chips"—battered pieces of cod or haddock, deep-fried and served with fries. The Indian food industry is worth £3.2

The ever popular fish and chips.

billion ($5.1 billion) and accounts for two-thirds of all takeouts. Made popular in the 1950s and 1960s, Chinese restaurants and take-out shops are waning in popularity due to the fact that many dishes are relatively simple to make at home. Take-out Thai cooking is another favorite, and, of course, pizza is ubiquitous.

Of the drinks consumed in Britain, by far the largest in quantity is tea. With a total population of over 63 million, Britons drink more than 165 million cups of tea daily! It was first imported in the seventeenth century, as was coffee, which has now become an important part of British lives. A recent survey revealed that tea sales are dropping but coffee is on the rise.

Tea time, with scones, jam, and clotted cream.

British beer has been popular since the invention of the brewing of hops, sugar, and yeast. The 2015 CAMRA (Campaign for Real Ale) Guide reports that there are 1,285 breweries operating in Britain, with an annual growth rate of over 10 percent. There is now one brewery for every 50,000 people! Drinkers tend to fall into two camps, with often the younger drinkers preferring the lighter lager beers—many of which are brewed out of the country—and drunk chilled, to the traditional bitter with its fuller flavor and drunk at room temperature.

REAL ALE

Founded in 1971, the CAMRA (Campaign for Real Ale) promotes real ale, real cider, and the traditional British pub in opposition to the mass production and **homogenization** of the British brewing industry. It produces an annual guide covering nearly 55,000 pubs with the 8,000 plus beers on offer, as well as a section listing every brewery—micro, regional, and national—that makes real ale in the UK.

Dark ale and pale ale.

Wine has increased in popularity since the 1950s, and today Britain imports more wine than any other country. Wines made in Britain account for just 1 percent of the country's consumption. There are around 475 vineyards producing predominantly white wines, although some make rosé and red wines. Many have won prestigious awards, much to the amazement of French wine producers!

Scottish whiskey.

Whisky is made in all countries of the United Kingdom but particularly in Scotland. The combination of water and fermented grain mash, of which barley is the most popular; the aging process; and the know-how of each producer, results in a flavor unique to each **distillery**. The spirit produced is only allowed to be called "whisky" after three years of aging, although single malts are aged for a minimum of eight years. Scotch whisky is exported to around 200 countries with forty bottles exported every second! It accounts for a quarter of UK food and drink exports.

While British food has a generally bad reputation out of the country—former French president Jacques Chirac famously said, "One cannot trust people whose cuisine is so bad"—this reputation is unfounded. One can eat very well with a huge variety of tastes and flavors accompanied by a cup of tea, or a glass of beer or wine, and followed by a "tot" of whisky!

Visitors at the scotch distillery in Dalwhinnie, Scotland.

TEXT-DEPENDENT QUESTIONS

1. Name and describe two of the most popular regional dishes in the UK.

2. What is the reason that Chinese take-out food is not as popular as it once was?

3. What is the most popular beverage in Britain?

RESEARCH PROJECTS

1. Select one regional specialty and find a recipe online for it. Prepare a menu for a meal based on the dish and a shopping list, noting any special equipment you might need.

2. Use the library and Internet to research one of the immigrant groups that has influenced British food. Write a brief report about the history of the immigrant group and how it keeps its home culture alive through its food.

A cherry-filled Bakewell tart.

The annual boat race between Cambridge and Oxford universities in 2009.

WORDS TO UNDERSTAND

mechanized: characterized by the use of machinery.

proximity: closeness or nearness in terms of location.

recession: an economic slowdown that usually causes businesses to falter and unemployment to increase.

sector: part or aspect of something, especially of a country's or region's economy.

CHAPTER 4

School, Work, and Industry

Despite an economic downturn that began in 2008 with the worldwide **recession**, Britain is still a vibrant country in which to live and work. An outstanding education system, world-renowned universities, interesting and varied job opportunities, and world-class international companies all contribute to its standing as the sixth largest economy in the world.

Children in the United Kingdom must receive full-time education between the ages of five and eighteen; however, some parents choose to send their children to kindergarten or preschool, where they are taught basic language and math skills. The compulsory education is divided into primary (from ages five to eleven) and secondary (from twelve to eighteen), with the last two years spent specializing in three to five subjects leading to A Level exams.

DRESSING IN BLUE

Uniforms were introduced to a large number of schools during the reign of King Henry VIII (1509–1507). As blue was the cheapest dye available, the early uniforms consisted of blue jackets and were known as "bluecoats." In 1870 the Elementary Education Act made education available for all children in England and Wales. Uniforms became more and more popular, until most schools required a uniform.

Around 93 percent of children attend state-funded schools with no fees apart from extracurricular activities like field trips, theatre excursions, and sports activities. The government funds these schools through taxation. The other 7 percent of pupils attend independent or private schools, some of which, for historical reasons, are known as "public schools." Requiring tuition, these are mostly day schools although some still require students to live on campus.

Prior to the nineteenth century, most schools segregated the sexes, with boys and girls taught in separate rooms, buildings, or even schools. Today they are relatively rare, although Great Britain still has over 10 percent of its schools operating as either all-girl or all-boy.

A guide at the Tower of London talks to a group of British schoolchildren.

More students than ever go to universities. In the 1970s around 5 percent of secondary graduates attend higher education, while the figure for today is over 35 percent, despite high tuition fees of up to £9,000 ($14,400). More girls than boys enroll in universities (55 percent to 45 percent), although it varies by the type of university. Imperial College London is a science, medicine, engineering, and business institution and has almost two-thirds male students, but universities specializing in art and design have predominantly female students.

Other courses of study dominated by women include veterinary science, with an incredible 52 percent increase in women studying in the field.

The costs of running universities are not completely covered by the tuition fees from British students, and so institutions aggressively recruit in foreign countries, especially in East Asia. A walk around a campus these days will reveal students from many countries, including South Korea, China, Japan, and Malaysia. Of course, this is reciprocated with British students attending foreign universities as well. And language students are more or less obliged to spend time studying abroad.

Oxford and Cambridge—known together as Oxbridge—are perhaps the two best-known universities in the world. And there has always been a great rivalry between the two. Oxford is the older institution, with evidence of teaching going back to 1096. In 1167 King Henry II banned students from studying at the University of Paris, and as a result Oxford University grew quickly after that. Following a quarrel with the town in 1209, some academics went northeast to set up what was to become Cambridge University. Oxford has many notable alumni, including twenty-seven Nobel Prize winners and twenty-six British prime ministers, while Cambridge boasts ninety Nobel Prize winners and fifteen prime ministers.

Cambridge University exterior.

Exterior view of Oxford University.

COMPETITION ON THE THAMES

In addition to other Oxford-Cambridge sporting events, the most famous is the annual boat race rowed over 4.2 miles (6.8 km) of the River Thames in London. Apart from during World War I and World War II, the race has run continuously since 1829, with Cambridge victorious eighty-one times and Oxford seventy-eight times . . . with one dead heat.

With their education completed, most people look for a job. As in the United States, substantial student loans can often burden students well into their professional lives. These could total £53,000 ($85,000), so some people are well into their fifties by the time they have repaid the total. The 65 percent of students who don't go on to university not only get a four-year start on the earning ladder, but they are also debt-free. In fact, some highly skilled blue-collar jobs, such as plumbers, electricians, and welders, can be very high-earning occupations.

Small- and medium-sized enterprises account for 99.9 percent of private-**sector** businesses and 60 percent of private-sector employment, with just under a fifth operating in the construction sector. The service sector—

which contributes nearly 80 percent of the country's economic output—is important in the small-business category and includes the many local shops and restaurants that keep towns and cities humming, both for the local population and travelers.

Tourism is indeed a major sector in Great Britain's economy. This includes, of course, the major cities, especially London, despite its high prices, but smaller cities and towns as well, including Edinburgh in Scotland and Shakespeare's birthplace, Stratford-upon-Avon in central England. The countryside also attracts travelers, including Brits as well as foreigners. With its many castles, gardens, and scenic seaside villages, Britain's economy is fed by visitors hoping to catch a glimpse of Britain's fabled past and take in its legendary hospitality.

On the other end of the service sector, London is still one of the major financial centers of the world. With high-tech infrastructure and well-educated businesspeople in the workforce, the headquarters of major international banking, investment, and insurers thrive in the UK. HSBC, Barclay, Lloyds, and the Royal Bank of Scotland are prominent examples.

The forces of globalization are at work in manufacturing, as well as the financial sector. And this has resulted in an erosion of Britain's manufacturing base, which has dropped dramatically since the early twentieth century, when heavy industry such as steel production and machine making were still an important part of the economy. Manufacturing now represents just 8 percent of the country's workforce and 12 percent of its national output.

Downtown London, May 2014.

A vintage 1936 Rolls-Royce at the Grand Prix in Mutschellen, Switzerland, 2012.

The car industry is the largest contributor to manufacturing output and is also one of the biggest examples of globalization in the British economy. Many traditionally iconic British auto companies are now largely owned by overseas companies: Jaguar-Land Rover by the Indian company Tata; Lotus by DRB-HICOM from Malaysia; Vauxhall by the American General Motors. Representing regional, European integration, Mini and Rolls-Royce are owned by the German company BMW and Bentley by the German Volkswagen. That said, major British auto brands still have operations in the United Kingdom. While owned by the German company Volkswagen, for instance, Bentley is still largely based in England, on the outskirts of Crewe, in Cheshire, England. East Asian companies, such as Honda, Toyota, and Nissan, all have factories in the UK as well.

COMMUTING

Many Britons travel long distances to get to work, with some taking the car to the station, a train into a city, followed by a ride on the subway, and finally a walk to the office. The average time taken is nearly an hour.

British farming, which employs only 1.5 percent of the labor force, has undergone major changes in the last thirty years, as it is now highly **mechanized** and intensive. Still, with a large and growing population, 40 percent of the country's food has to be imported. A shift to organic farming, however, has made for a more labor-intensive business and spurred younger people's interest in farming as a way of life. Varying types of agriculture—grains, livestock, fruits, and vegetables—flourish in the UK due mainly to the wide range of climates, soils, and topographies, as well as proximity to markets.

Referred to as the "underground" or the "tube," London's subway system is one of the most extensive in the world.

TEXT-DEPENDENT QUESTIONS

1. Describe the levels of schooling in Britain.

2. Name one factor that makes tourism an important sector of the British economy.

3. What were the most important types of manufacturing in the early twentieth century in Britain and what are they today?

RESEARCH PROJECTS

1. Use the library or Internet to research the history of Oxford or Cambridge University. Make a time line of important dates in the history of the university.

2. Select one of the auto manufacturing companies that still operates in the UK. Write a brief report on the company, including its history, where its facilities are, and what its most popular auto makes and models are. Include pictures of the cars.

Tourists enjoying sightseeing in London.

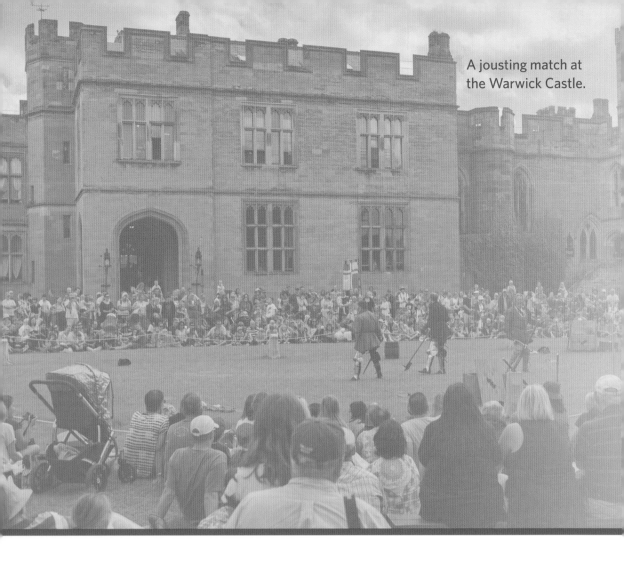

A jousting match at the Warwick Castle.

WORDS TO UNDERSTAND

atmospheric: in art, relating to a hazy quality, making the atmosphere visible.

controversial: provoking disagreement.

conventional: dull and unadventurous; bound to tradition.

prolific: highly productive, usually of intellectual or artistic work.

wane: grow smaller; lessen.

CHAPTER 5

Arts and Entertainment

The British people embrace a wide range of art forms and entertainment. Art, books, music, film, theater, and sports—a multitude of entertainment can be had wherever you go in the country.

Britain has been the birthplace of many great artists and architects and is the home of some of the world's best art galleries. Arguably the United Kingdom's greatest painter, whose work shaped eighteenth-century art on both sides of the Atlantic, was J. M. W. (Joseph Mallord William) Turner. Born in 1775, Turner was considered **controversial** in his day but is now thought of as one of the greatest masters of both oil and watercolor painting.

Wreckers Coast of Northumberland, by J. M. W. Turner, oil on canvas (1834).

The Pre-Raphaelite Brotherhood—a group of painters who objected to the influence of Sir Joshua Reynolds, the founder of the Royal Academy of Arts—was founded in 1848. Thinking Reynolds was too **conventional**, the Brotherhood wanted to revitalize British art. Members included John Everett Millais and Dante Gabriel Rossetti.

 MASTER OF LIGHT

J. M. W. Turner was a great experimenter in the use of paints and is sometimes called "the painter of light." He often painted landscapes with vivid sunsets and other engaging **atmospheric** conditions, such as fog and sea spray. Many of his finest works are displayed at the Tate Gallery in London.

Self-Portrait, by J. M. W. Turner, oil on canvas (ca. 1798).

Often considered one of Britain's greatest living artists, David Hockney was born in Bradford, West Yorkshire, in the northwest of England in 1937. He has works in oils, acrylics, and watercolors, as well as printmaking, photography, and theatrical set designs. He is quick to embrace new technology, painting portraits, still lifes, and landscapes using the app "Brushes" on iPhone and iPad. Other, more controversial artists of the later twentieth century include Damian Hurst, who has produced works that include animals preserved in formaldehyde and a work entitled *For the Love of God*, a human skull created in platinum and encrusted with £15,000,000 ($24,000,000) worth of diamonds!

Britain has also produced famous and ground-breaking writers. Geoffrey Chaucer (ca. 1343–1400), universally thought of as the greatest English poet of the Middle Ages, is often considered the Father of English Literature. Although best known for his *Canterbury Tales*, he was a **prolific** writer and was the first to be buried in Poet's Corner in Westminster Abbey, London.

William Shakespeare is Britain's most famous writer. Born in 1564, he wrote thirty-eight plays, as well as sonnets, epic poems, and other poetic works during his fifty-two years. Translated into all major languages, his plays, such as *Romeo and Juliet* and *Hamlet*, are the most performed of any playwright.

Jane Austen's work was little known in her lifetime (1775–1817) but gained popularity later in the nineteenth century, and even more so in the twentieth century. Considered literary classics, her novels include *Sense and Sensibility* and *Pride and Prejudice*. Roughly of the same era, the poets John Keats, Lord Byron, and Percy Bysshe Shelley are regarded as some of the finest in the English language, as is novelist Charles Dickens, whose classics form part of the curriculum of many high school students in the English-speaking world. Dickens' first writings were originally published in monthly installments in magazines. His first novel, *Oliver Twist*, was very well received and his followers couldn't wait for each installment to appear.

THE EAGLE AND CHILD

A pub with a tiny front door in Oxford called the Eagle and Child played host to two writers who met regularly at lunchtime on a Monday or Tuesday. They were C. S. Lewis, who went on to publish the seven books that made up *The Chronicles of Narnia*, and J. R. R. Tolkien, the author of *The Hobbit* and *The Lord of the Rings*.

Britain's classical music has drawn heavily on church music and to a certain extent folk traditions. One prominent example is George Frideric Handel, who was born in Germany in 1685 but became a naturalized British subject in 1727. He wrote operas, oratorios, anthems, and

The Eagle and Child pub in Oxford, England.

organ concertos including *Messiah*, a popular work sung in both the Christmas and Easter seasons in many countries across the world.

American popular musicians, including Perry Como and Frankie Laine, dominated Britain in the early 1950s, but by the late 1950s English groups started to emerge, particularly in Liverpool in the northwest

A vintage Beatles stamp.

of England. It is said that at least 350 bands were playing in the city in the late 1950s and early 1960s. And by the mid-1960s, the "British Invasion" of the United States occurred, led by the Beatles and followed by bands such as the Dave Clark Five, Kinks, Rolling Stones, and The Who.

Formed in Liverpool in 1960, the Beatles became probably the greatest and most influential group in rock and pop history. They started playing in clubs in Liverpool, most notably the Cavern Club, but soon went to Hamburg in Germany, returning to Britain in 1962 to record their first disk, "Love Me Do," which peaked at number seventeen in the charts. This was followed by "Please Please Me," which pushed the band to almost instant fame in Britain and the United States. Since then, they regularly issued albums that were eagerly awaited by fans across the world, with the last one, *Abbey Road*, released in 1969.

Boy bands including Take That and East 17, and girl bands, such as the Spice Girls, became popular, although at the end of the century, their popularity began to **wane**. Solo female artists continued to succeed, however, with powerful voices such as Amy Winehouse, Adele, and Duffy achieving success on both sides of the Atlantic.

THE EDINBURGH FESTIVAL

Taking place in the summer in Edinburgh, Scotland, the Edinburgh Festival is in fact a collection of events organized by different people. Together they form the largest annual cultural festival in the world. It showcases exponents of theater, comedy, and writing and is often a springboard for new talent.

The British theater industry has produced many international stars and continues to entertain people all over the country. In the land of Shakespeare, one is never far away from some of the most varied theater in the world. Plays such as *Charley's Aunt*, whose original London run tallied a record-breaking 1,466 performances, *Look Back in Anger*, and *The Rocky Horror Show* have all traveled to other countries while also delighting British audiences. Britain's film industry has continued to entertain since the beginnings of cinema with the two highest-grossing film series ever—*Harry Potter* and *James Bond*—both based on books by British authors and both made in Britain.

The most popular leisure activity in Britain is watching television, with a per capita viewing time of four hours per day. Favorite programs include activities much cherished by Britons, such as wildlife documentaries, cooking programs, gardening, and sports. Britain's television drama is still considered some of the best in the world. And series, such as *Downton Abbey*, can regularly be seen in other countries, including the United States.

A stilt walker entertains the crowd during the Edinburgh Festival, August 2012.

FORMULA ONE IN BRITAIN AND BEYOND

Of the eleven motor-racing teams that began the 2014 Formula One season, eight are based in Britain—such is the wealth of automotive-design talent in the UK. Among the eight, only one team operates away from the immediate environs of the Silverstone Circuit, one of the epicenters of motorsports in the UK. The British teams compete all around the world and are ambassadors of British know-how.

Britain is a keen watcher, if not player, of sport. Football (soccer) is avidly followed, with one of the most famous clubs, Manchester United, getting regular attendances of 75,000 fans. Since Britain hosted the summer Olympics in 2012, interest in sports and athletics has risen dramatically, including cycling, rowing, and sailing, with individual players achieving star status, such as Mo Farrah, Jessica Ennis, and Andy Murray. Ben Ainslie, the most successful sailor in Olympic history, won medals in five successive summer Olympics, with gold medals in the last four.

Manchester United, in white, play in the UEFA Champions League F Group at the Turkish Telecom Arena in Istanbul.

TEXT-DEPENDENT QUESTIONS

1. Who was George Frideric Handel?

2. Where did the Beatles get their start?

3. What soccer team is the most popular in Britain?

RESEARCH PROJECTS

1. Find an image of one of J. M. W. Turner's paintings on the Internet or in the library and describe it, including what is actually in the painting as well as the style in which it was painted and the qualities and feelings it conveys.

2. Compare one of the top sports stars or teams mentioned in the chapter to one of your own favorites. Use the library or Internet for your research and outline what you find in a table.

A mummer, or actor, holds the Wassail blessing at the Globe Theatre in London.

GLOBE WASSAIL
Blowe Winde, Globe bear well,
Spring well in playing.
Every Lathe & every Timber
Bear the tongues of Poets
Next New Year's Summer!

Spanish Fly

A village on the River Nidd in Knaresborough, North Yorkshire.

WORDS TO UNDERSTAND

follies: structures, usually in gardens, that are used for leisure and are often fanciful in their design.

heritage: tradition and history.

Jurassic: dating from the period of the dinosaurs, starting some 208 million years ago.

longitude: the distance between a point on any meridian and the Prime Meridian at Greenwich.

CHAPTER 6

Cities, Towns, and the Countryside

Despite being a small country, Britain has a range of different geographical features: miles of coastline, low flat plains, rolling hills, and ragged mountains. All these help to determine the location and character of villages, towns, and cities. History has had its part to play as well: towns form around strategic defense posts and cities rise due to their importance in manufacture and commerce. These many and varied sites in the UK attest to the country's importance regionally and on the wold stage—both historically and in the present day.

The largest city in the United Kingdom is England's capital, London. It has a population of just over 8.5 million. One other city has a population greater than a million and that distinction goes to Birmingham in the Midlands. Just three others have populations of over 500,000—Leeds, Glasgow in Scotland, and Sheffield, in the northeast. The smallest designated city in the United Kingdom is St. Davids (or St. David's) in Wales with a population of just 1,797!

 ## DESIGNATING THE SMALLEST CITY

Kings and queens, not Parliament or the prime minister, grant localities the status of cities in the UK. The last resting place of Saint David, Wales's patron saint, St. Davids (or St. David's) was granted city status in the sixteenth century because of the existence of the cathedral, but it lost this right in 1888. In 1991 the town council asked for the designation to be restored on the occasion of the fortieth anniversary of the coronation of Queen Elizabeth II, who granted it in 1994.

Built on each side of the River Thames, London has a history dating back over 2,000 years. The Romans named it Londinium, and its heart, the City of London, keeps its boundaries as they were in medieval times. It had a resident population of just 7,375 in the 2011 census, making it the smallest city in England! However, since the nineteenth century, the metropolis surrounding this core has been referred to as London.

Now a major global city, London is one of the world's leading financial

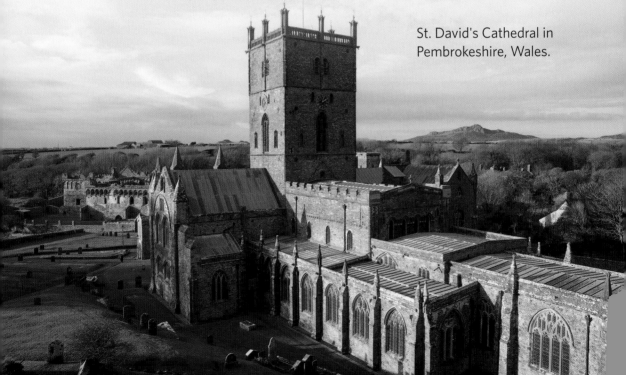

St. David's Cathedral in Pembrokeshire, Wales.

Aerial view of East London showing the Tower Bridge, Canary Wharf, City Hall, and the River Thames.

centers and also has a strong presence in the arts, commerce, education, and fashion. Measured by passenger traffic, it has the world's largest city airport system and is the world's most visited city based on international arrivals. It is internationally renowned for such buildings as Buckingham Palace, the Tower of London, and Westminster Abbey. The Palace of Westminster, one of Britain's best-known buildings, is the seat of the Houses of Commons and Lords, making up the Parliament of the United Kingdom.

Other well-known attractions are St. Paul's Cathedral, Tower Bridge, and the London Eye, which is a giant ferris wheel overlooking the Thames and the Palace of Westminster. Trafalgar Square and Piccadilly Circus are other famous gathering places. The presence of the Royal Family's principal residence, Buckingham Palace, and all the pomp and ceremony surrounding it, have contributed around £500 ($800) million every year in tourist revenue.

 GREENWICH AND THE MERIDIAN

King Charles II created the post of astronomer royal and commissioned the architect Sir Christopher Wren to design the Royal Observatory in the Royal Borough of Greenwich, which lies down the river from central London. The Prime **Meridian**—the origin (zero **longitude**) upon which all east-west distances around the world is based—was established in 1851. It is marked by a stainless steel strip laid down in the courtyard, and by night, a powerful green laser shines north across the River Thames.

Birmingham was a medium-sized market town in medieval times but grew in the latter half of the eighteenth century during the Industrial Revolution. While it does have large factories, it was the thousands of small, specialized workshops that led to the city's prosperity. Today its centralized position geographically makes it a key hub in the transport, retail, and conference sectors. Not only busi-

Steam rising off the hot mineral water at the Great Bath, in Bath, England.

nesses, but cultural institutions of international renown—such as the City of Birmingham Symphony Orchestra and the Birmingham Royal Ballet—make it a vital English city.

Leeds in West Yorkshire, another important English city, developed as a market town centered around the wool industry, and its growth was initially helped by the building of a network of canals and railways linking it to important ports such as Liverpool and Hull. Leeds also retained its links with agriculture in the growth of woolen and flax mills. International competition in manufacturing led the city to turn in the 1970s to the service sector. It is now a legal center (second only to London) and, with connection to the electronic and telecommunication infrastructure, a telephone banking center.

Bath in the southwest of England is named after the hot spring baths established by the Romans. It became popular as a spa town in Georgian times, and

The Royal Crescent of Georgian-style houses in Bath.

many fine buildings remain from that era, including the beautiful Royal Crescent, the Circus (three blocks of houses forming a circle), and the Paragon (a row of Georgian-style houses). A social gathering spot called the Grand Pump Room was built in 1799, as a place to drink the water—supposedly giving health benefits—before it enters the hot Roman baths, which remain a major attraction.

The small seaside town of Whitby, in the north of England, developed as a fishing port in the Middle Ages and has several claims to fame. It was here that the explorer Captain James Cook first learned seamanship. He went on to make three voyages spanning the globe during the years from 1768 to 1779. Whitby is also noted for the novel *Dracula* by Bram Stoker. Following the running aground of a crewless Russian ship off Whitby, an animal resembling "a large dog" is seen leaping ashore—Dracula has arrived in Britain!

TWINNING

To encourage tourism and trade, towns can apply to "twin" with towns in other countries. The practice appeared just after World War II as a way of fostering friendship and peace between former enemies. An example is Coventry in the Midlands, which twinned with both Stalingrad and Dresden, as all were heavily bombed during the war. The idea has spread to the United States, although the term "sister city" is more widely used. For instance, a town in Scotland called Dull is twinned with Boring, Oregon!

Historical preservation plays an important role in maintaining the UK's **heritage**. For instance, the Landmark Trust rescues important buildings that would otherwise be lost. It owns 200 buildings and its funding comes from renting them for vacations. One can stay in castles, **follies**, unused stations, a water tower, a hospital, and even a summer house built in the shape of a pineapple!

The United Kingdom's diverse geography has made the physical appearance of towns and villages quite distinctive, the local stone lending different colors to the buildings throughout the country. The Cotswolds in south-central

England contain the rolling Cotswold Hills, made from **Jurassic** limestone, and the buildings shine a golden yellow in the sun. In towns of Scotland, the rock is a dark, forbidding granite, whereas towns around the Midlands are mainly built of brick. Such varied richness gives the UK's physical environments a beauty and interest, worth exploring from one end to the other.

The front façade of the Dunmore House in Scotland.

Cotswold hamlet of Hailes in Gloucestershire, England.

TEXT-DEPENDENT QUESTIONS

1. Under whose authority are localities granted the status of cities?
2. What are the origins of the UK's capital, London?
3. According to the chapter, what is one way Britain's historical legacy is preserved?

RESEARCH PROJECTS

1. Research the history of one of the cities mentioned in the chapter and create a timeline of the major events that helped give the city its current shape and importance.
2. Draw a rough map of Great Britain and on it chart the course of the River Thames and other inland water features. Plot the major cities and sites of the country—both mentioned in the chapter and those not. Then, consulting with sources in the library and on the Internet, write one to two paragraphs about one of those sites or cities and its relationship to the surrounding environment.

The White Cliffs of Dover.

FURTHER RESEARCH

Online

The Central Intelligence Agency's World Fact Book on the United Kingdom (https://www.cia.gov/library/publications/the-world-factbook/geos/uk.html) provides current statistics and basic information about the UK's government, economy, demographics, and culture.

The website about the UK's National Trust (http://www.nationaltrust.org.uk/) offers general information about its mission and history, plus details about the properties and structures it protects.

The UK government website (www.gov.uk) covers basic information on aspects of living in the country, such as driving, education, and voting.

Books

Easton, Mark. *Britain Etc.* New York: Simon & Schuster, 2012.

Frase, Rebecca. *The Story of Britain: From the Romans to the Present: A Narrative History.* New York: Norton, 2006.

Fuller, Barbara. *Cultures of the World: Great Britain.* New York: Cavendish Square, 2005.

Hall, Geoff. *British Stuff: Life in Britain Through 101 Everyday Objects.* Chichester, UK: Summersdale, 2013.

Mason, Laura. *Food Culture in Great Britain.* Westport, CT: Greenwood, 2004.

NOTE TO EDUCATORS: This book contains both imperial and metric measurements as well as references to global practices and trends in an effort to encourage the student to gain a worldly perspective. We, as publishers, feel it's our role to give young adults the tools they need to thrive in a global society.

SERIES GLOSSARY

ancestral: relating to ancestors, or relatives who have lived in the past.

archaeologist: a scientist that investigates past societies by digging in the earth to examine their remains.

artisanal: describing something produced on a small scale, usually handmade by skilled craftspeople.

colony: a settlement in another country or place that is controlled by a "home" country.

commonwealth: an association of sovereign nations unified by common cultural, political, and economic interests and traits.

communism: a social and economic philosophy characterized by a classless society and the absence of private property.

continent: any of the seven large land masses that constitute most of the dry land on the surface of the earth.

cosmopolitan: worldly; showing the influence of many cultures.

culinary: relating to the kitchen, cookery, and style of eating.

cultivated: planted and harvested for food, as opposed to the growth of plants in the wild.

currency: a system of money.

demographics: the study of population trends.

denomination: a religious grouping within a faith that has its own organization.

dynasty: a ruling family that extends across generations, usually in an autocratic form of government, such as a monarchy.

ecosystems: environments where interdependent organisms live.

endemic: native, or not introduced, to a particular region, and not naturally found in other areas.

exile: absence from one's country or home, usually enforced by a government for political or religious reasons.

feudal: a system of economic, political, or social organization in which poor landholders are subservient to wealthy landlords; used mostly in relation to the Middle Ages.

globalization: the processes relating to increasing international exchange that have resulted in faster, easier connections across the world.

gross national product: the measure of all the products and services a country produces in a year.

heritage: tradition and history.

homogenization: the process of blending elements together, sometimes resulting in a less interesting mixture.

iconic: relating to something that has become an emblem or symbol.

idiom: the language particular to a community or class; usually refers to regular, "everyday" speech.

immigrants: people who move to and settle in a new country.

indigenous: originating in and naturally from a particular region or country.

industrialization: the process by which a country changes from a farming society to one that is based on industry and manufacturing.

SERIES GLOSSARY

integration: the process of opening up a place, community, or organization to all types of people.

kinship: web of social relationships that have a common origin derived from ancestors and family.

literacy rate: the percentage of people who can read and write.

matriarchal: of or relating to female leadership within a particular group or system.

migrant: a person who moves from one place to another, usually for reasons of employment or economic improvement.

militarized: warlike or military in character and thought.

missionary: one who goes on a journey to spread a religion.

monopoly: a situation where one company or state controls the market for an industry or product.

natural resources: naturally occurring materials, such as oil, coal, and gold, that can be used by people.

nomadic: describing a way of life in which people move, usually seasonally, from place to place in search of food, water, and pastureland.

nomadic: relating to people who have no fixed residence and move from place to place.

parliament: a body of government responsible for enacting laws.

patriarchal: of or relating to male leadership within a particular group or system.

patrilineal: relating to the relationship based on the father or the descendants through the male line.

polygamy: the practice of having more than one spouse.

provincial: belonging to a province or region outside of the main cities of a country.

racism: prejudice or animosity against people belonging to other races.

ritualize: to mark or perform with specific behaviors or observances.

sector: part or aspect of something, especially of a country's or region's economy.

secular: relating to worldly concerns; not religious.

societal: relating to the order, structure, or functioning of society or community.

socioeconomic: relating to social and economic factors, such as education and income, often used when discussing how classes, or levels of society, are formed.

statecraft: the ideas about and methods of running a government.

traditional: relating to something that is based on old historical ways of doing things.

urban sprawl: the uncontrolled expansion of urban areas away from the center of the city into remote, outlying areas.

urbanization: the increasing movement of people from rural areas to cities, usually in search of economic improvement, and the conditions resulting this migration.

INDEX

Italicized page numbers refer to illustrations.

INDEX

INDEX

INDEX

PHOTO CREDITS

Page	Page Location	Archive/Photographer	Page	Page Location	Archive/Photographer
6	Full page	Dreamstime/Ultra67	32	Top	Dreamstime/Patrickwang
8	Top	Dreamstime/Michal Bednarek	34	Middle	Dreamstime/Jim Kelcher
10	Top	Dollar Photo Club/Simon Gurney	35	Bottom	Dreamstime/Nicolae Gherasim
11	Bottom right	Wikimedia Commons/Google Cultural Institute	36	Top	Dreamstime/Jennifer Barrow
12	Bottom right	Wikimedia Commons/Paul Mellon Collection in the Yale Center for British Art	37	Bottom	Dreamstime/Stanko07
			38	Top left	Dreamstime/Martin Lehmann
			38	Bottom right	Dreamstime/Peter Spirer
13	Top right	Dreamstime/Davidmartyn	39	Bottom	Dreamstime/Martinmark
14	Bottom right	Wikimedia Commons/J. McNeven	40	Top	Dreamstime/Stanko07
15	Bottom	Dreamstime/Clickos	42	Top	Wikimedia Commons/Joseph Mallord William Turner
16	Top	Dreamstime/Alenmax	42	Middle	Wikimedia Commons/Joseph Mallord William Turner
19	Bottom	Dreamstime/Anizza			
21	Top right	Dreamstime/Dave Bredeson	43	Bottom right	Wikimedia Commons/MPerel
21	Bottom	Dreamstime/Sharad Raval	44	Top right	Dreamstime/Konstantin32
22	Bottom	Dreamstime/Jason Batterham	45	Bottom	Dreamstime/Jan Kranendonk
23	Bottom	Dreamstime/Danielal	46	Bottom	Dreamstime/Naci Yavuz
24	Top	Dreamstime/Ld1976d	47	Bottom	Dreamstime/Wendy Leber
26	Top	Dreamstime/Ppy2010ha	48	Top	Dreamstime/Androniques
27	Top right	Dreamstime/Philkinsey	50	Bottom	Dreamstime/Lian Deng
27	Bottom left	Dreamstime/Paul Cowan	51	Top	Dreamstime/Yolfran
28	Bottom	Dreamstime/Charlieaja	52	Top right	Dreamstime/Anthony Brown
29	Top right	Dreamstime/Anjelagr	52-53	Bottom	Dreamstime/Chris Lofty
29	Bottom right	Dreamstime/Steven Cukrov	54	Middle	Wikimedia Commons/giannandrea
30	Top right	Dreamstime/Chris Leachman	54	Bottom	Dreamstime/Andrew Roland
30	Bottom	Dreamstime/John Braid	55	Bottom	Dreamstime/Marco Saracco
31	Bottom	Dreamstime/Derek Phillips			

COVER

Top	Dollar Photo Club/kmiragaya
Bottom left	Dollar Photo Club/Debu55y
Bottom right	Dreamstime/Martin Molcan

ABOUT THE AUTHOR

Born and bred in the United Kingdom, **Richard Garratt** initially worked as a designer for the publishers Macmillan, David and Charles, and Oxford University Press before becoming a freelance designer and the design director for Curtis Garratt Limited—a small, independent design/editorial company specializing in the production of nonfiction books.

With the rise of computer-based production methods and the ease of file transferral, he seized the opportunity to live and work in France, where he specializes in providing high-quality content for a wide range of nonfiction publications, including illustrations and maps for encyclopedias and other reference works.

A publishing all-rounder, Richard has worked for many clients in the United States, the United Kingdom, France, and Japan.